MASSEL SMITH

My Mother Sleeps
My Journey

Copyright @2020 by Massel Smith

All rights reserved. No part of this book may be reproduced in any form or by any electronic or mechanical means, including information storage and retrieval systems, without permission in writing from the publisher, except by reviewers, who may quote brief passages in a review.

This publication contains the opinions and ideas of its author. It is intended to provide helpful and informative material on the subjects addressed in the publication. The author and publisher specifically disclaim all responsibility for any liability, loss or risk, personal or otherwise, which is incurred as a consequence, directly or indirectly, of the use and application of any of the contents of this book.

WORKBOOK PRESS LLC
187 E Warm Springs Rd,
Suite B285, Las Vegas, NV 89119, USA

Website: https://workbookpress.com/
Hotline: 1-888-818-4856
Email: admin@workbookpress.com

Ordering Information:
Quantity sales. Special discounts are available on quantity purchases by corporations, associations, and others.
For details, contact the publisher at the address above.

ISBN-13: 978-1-952754-83-8 (Paperback Version)
978-1-952754-84-5 (Digital Version)

REV. DATE: 04/09/2020

TABLE OF CONTENTS

CHAPTER 1
    1944 9
    MY PAPA 10

CHAPTER 2
    MAMA SLEEP 11
    THE GENTLE ONE 13

CHAPTER 3
    A NEW WIFE 14

CHAPTER 4
    PORTRIOT 16

CHAPTER 5
    BIG CITY 17

CHAPTER 6
    MOTHER 19

CHAPTER 7
    IT WAS SATURDAY 20

CHAPTER 8
    TERROR 22

CHAPTER 9
    LIFE IN A NEW WAY 23

CHAPTER 10
    SCHOOL DAYS 24

CHAPTER 11
    COURAGE 25

CHAPTER 12
    RED DRESS 27

CHAPTER 13
    NO PERFECT PERSON 28

CHAPTER 14
    QUEENS HIGH SCHOOL 30

CHAPTER 15
    TEENAGE YEARS 32

CHAPTER 16
    LIVING WITH SISTER VALERIE 34

CHAPTER 17
    LEAVING MY LAND OF BIRTH 36

CHAPTER 18
    MONTREAL 38

CHAPTER 19
    THE GROWTH OF A WOMAN 40

CHAPTER 20
    BROKEN WINGS 41

CHAPTER 21
    TIME TO MOVE ON 42

CHAPTER 22
    LEAVING NEW YORK 43

CHAPTER 23
    THE DECISION 45

CHAPTER 24
    TWO JOBS 46

CHAPTER 25
    ONE NEVER KNOWS 48

CHAPTER 26
    DEAR MASSELL 51

CHAPTER 27
    THE JOY OF LIVING 52

CHAPTER 28
    THE THINGS WE FACE IN LIFE 53

CHAPTER 29
    BE AWAKE 54

CHAPTER 30
    BONDED BY BIRTH 55

CHAPTER 31
    LIFE HAS CHEATED ME .58

CHAPTER 32
    THE SILHOUETTE ON THE HILL 60

CHAPTER 33
    MY THREE WISHES 62

CHAPTER 34
    DINNER WITH MAMA 63

CHAPTER 35
    THOUGHTS ON FRIENDSHIP .64

CHAPTER 36
    TO BE STRONG 65

CHAPTER 37
    THE MAN WITH THE GOLDEN VOICE 66

CHAPTER 38
    LETTER TO MY SELF 67

CHAPTER 39
    THE JOURNEY TO SURGERY 68

CHAPTER 40
    THE APHASIA INSTITUTE AND PAT ARATO
    CENTRE 70

CHAPTER 41
    MY APHASIA AND ME 71

CHAPTER 42
    A JOURNEY THROUGH THE FOREST 72

CHAPTER 43
    A ROSE GARDEN 75

CHAPTER 44
    THIS IS THE TIME SPRING 76

TO THE VOLUNTEERS 77

TO MY READERS 78

ACKNOWLEDGEMENT 80

Massel Smith

CHAPTER 1
April 1944

    1945 brings the end of World War ll. It was also the year after my birth. The world had turned upside down, people were coming home wounded. Some came home safely; others were sent home in boxes. It was a bittersweet time! They had nothing to look forward to. The war had killed their joy. But there was one home that was blessed with great joy.

    I came in this world on April 1, 1944. The family increased to five children. I was the baby and I was spoiled by everyone. Then three years later my baby sister was born, I was no longer the baby. My mom now did not have energy, she spent a lot of her time in bed. There was one thing she wanted to do for all of us. This was very important. She had made plans to have our portrait of the family taken. When the day arrived, she dressed us in our Sunday's best to go to church. The photographer came to our home and took our picture. It was Mama, Papa and the six children. Mama knew something that we did not know. It was not long after that, mama took ill. She spent most of her time in bed. Then one day, Papa called us to her bed side. She had something to say to us. As we were going to Mama's room my brother Eucal, dashed out of the house. I asked, "Where you are going?" "I am going to get aunty". No sooner that he said he was back with aunty. She did not hear well. We are now in mama's room I climbed onto her bed she told us she wanted to say goodbye to us. We asked her. "where are you going?", She was crying when she said, "I just have to go, not my will but my Heavenly Father's. He wants me home, I must go". Then she looked at our aunty, Winnie (our father's sister) she said "Winnie, here is your daughter as she handed her the baby. (Eulice) Take good care of her". She turned to us as her tears flowed and said "I love you all so much, but my time has come. I have to go." I asked "But where are you going?" She turned and said "One day you will know." We were upset every one of us. I think we all cried ourselves to sleep. Next morning Mama slept the eternal sleep of death.

My Mother Sleeps

How does a man watched his wife; each day each night. Knowing she is going. Will it be today, tonight or tomorrow? What can he say to their kids? His face smeared with agony; as he watched her sleep. What can he say to their kids, to erase the pain of her leaving? He must be strong for them. What can I truly say? He wiped the tears from his eyes. What will he do? He will be strong for the kids. Tomorrow is another day.

MY PAPA

How does a man with a heart full of love for his Wife and children feel.
Day after day he knew she would be leaving him forever.
Will be today, tonight or tomorrow?
Could he have seen the future? Would it have made a difference?
His children were all under twelve years old.
What would happen to them?

He wiped the tears from his eyes, as he sits beside her bed.
He is now a broken man, his wife is gone forever.
The pain in his heart could be seen in his eyes. But yet he kept going on for his children, that is what she would have wanted.
His faith in God would not fail. A quite man was he, he saw no evil and he did no evil to anyone.
Yet he would be tested time and time again.
His faith would see him through each hurdle.

CHAPTER 2
Mama sleep

Mama was gone but life goes on for the rest of us. Not fully understanding what was going on, I was afraid my Papa would go away too. At nights I would not go to sleep until I saw my Papa; then I would know he was not leaving us. Likewise in the mornings, he was the first one I would call for. Not hearing him I would dash out of the house crying at the top of my lungs, calling "Papa! Papa!" I did not care that the grass was taller than me or the rain was falling, I had to get to the pasture where Papa and my brothers.

Boyd and Eucal were milking the cows. The milk had to be out by seven in the morning so the milk truck could take it to the milk factory in Bog Walk. There was a river that I would have to cross over to the other side. That's where the pasture was. I did not think that the river might be moving too fast or that it might overflow its banks, I just had to find papa. He would leave the milking and come to get me before I get to the river.

Another thing, I had to be ready for school by 7:30 a.m. of course, I did not want to go because that meant I would leave papa and I did not know if I would see him anymore. He might go away like Mama did. So, I would start my crying; jumping up; scratching myself; and screaming "Lord, Jesus Christ." I would not even move one step. I was just not going to go to school. I have to stay with Papa. Would he be here when I returned? I did not want my papa out of my sight, for then I would know he was not going to leave me.

The kindergarten and the big school were in the same building. The kindergarten was at the west end and the upper classes were at the east end of the building. The upper classes also occupied the upstairs. The kindergarten was out before the big school. So, I would climb the stairs and stand at the door of his class as I waited for my brother. Eucal was a bit embarrassed. His friends would say, "Look who is at the door –

your sister." Then one evening his teacher invited me in. I was in my seventh heaven. No sooner I was in the room, I presumed to tell them my brother combed my hair. See how beautifully he put my ribbons, and I was turning this way and that way. The class was laughing, and then the teacher asked a questioned, one student was standing to give the answer. Then I said as I pointed to one student after another, "You too and you," then I open my arms wide saying "All of you stand up, all of you". The whole class was in stitches. They were laughing so hard. The only one who was not laughing was my brother Eucal. The lessons stopped there. The class was over for the day. Now, when I think back it was quite funny. That was the only morning I did not make a fuss to go to school.

Eucal is the gentle one, just like papa. He never gets cross with any one nor says anything to hurt anyone. If he had a game of cricket after school, my sister Heather and I would wait for him. We go to school together and we go home together.

I have never seen our Papa mad at any of us except for this one time. Now that I am thinking of the incident it was quite laughable. My brothers, Boyd and Eucal and their friend Trevor would go every Sundays to the river for a swim. The river runs through my uncle's property. There is a spot in the river where they can dive off the rocks. It was very secluded a beautiful and calm area. They would not let anyone outside of the district swim there but there was this one man who did not live in the district who would come every Sunday for a swim. My brothers and Trevor told him time and time again to stop coming there. He refused to stop. So this Sunday in question when the boys got there, the man was there. So what do you think they did? They took his clothes and hid them, so when he got out of the water there were no clothes. Sometime in the afternoon we – my sisters and I were outside then we heard papa saying, "Get in the house". We could not understand what was going on but we were soon to find out. We look through the door and there was this man coming through our kitchen garden no clothes on. What a sight to behold! That was the only time I saw our papa get upset with any of us. It was quite hilarious. I suppose that man got the message the hard way.

Massel Smith

I was always afraid of the dark so as the twilight hour crept in I would not go out of the house by myself I could see the birds flying and singing as they looked for a place to rest their tired wings. This time of the day is very quite and serenity takes over.

THE GENTLE ONE

Brother! Oh brother of mine,
Your gentle voice gives me courage.
I see our Papa in you.
Never having a bad word for anyone.
Your gentleness is like a clean clear stream,
Meandering through the lily patch on its way down stream.

I see the gentleness you showed to our dear sister Heather.
In the last days of her life.
May happiness and peace be yours always.
Dear brother,
You are truly our father's son.

My Mother Sleeps

CHAPTER 3
A New Wife

I think it wasn't long after Mama's death that my father got a new wife. She was quite attractive and had children. I thought we were getting a new mother, but how wrong I was! She was never a mother to any of us. Remember the question my older sister had asked our father "Papa are we going to get another Mama?" That question has never left my mind, it is with me always.

I was the youngest one at home I cannot remember her giving me bath or brushing my hair. Instead, I was doing chores that were bigger than me. I had to go to the springs to fetch water. On the Island in those days, we did not have running water. The springs and rivers, that's where our God – given water came from. Also, there were homes that collected it from the rain by building tanks and big drums have a shaft leading in the tank from the roof. On my way to the spring I would call my sister, Eulice. She lived a few steps from the spring. The spring was on our uncle's property. She would come hopping and skipping down the path. We would play chasing butterflies across the field. Time seem to stop for us. Those were happy times, moments that will stay with me throughout my life.

There were times when I had to iron my little brother and sister clothes that were too big for me. I would watch my big sisters as they were ironing. They would place the iron over their hand to see if it was hot. To iron, we had to use the coal stove. The stove would take four irons that were so ancient compared to now. I would iron in the kitchen. The kitchen was not joined to the house. When our stepmother was away, my sisters would do everything for me. They saw me as the baby. One day I had to do ironing. I wanted to do what my sisters did. I took the iron from the stove and placed it on my skin. Don't asked me what I did. I placed the iron on my skin. I saw the sun, the moon, and the stars all rolled into one. The pain was sheer agony. It took a long time to heal, but I learned my lesson in a painful way. I will carry that scar for the rest of my life. My stepmother did haggling so she would go to other farmer's fields and buy the goods. Sometimes my old sister and I would have to go to those farms and get the goods so, we would have to miss school. That did not seem to worry her not at all as long as she got her way. My dad did not stop her. Not only did I have to go to the farms, but sometimes I would have to spend the night at the market. Most people would come to the market on Friday evening, and on those days, I had to go to a private school for girls. By the way I had no shoes on and the soles of my feet were a complete mess from those sharp stones. As a mother, my stepmother did nothing. We are not her kids. My aunt that lives in the USA came for holidays. She saw my feet and was very upset. So, when she got home she sent lots of things to all of us. Once, my aunt sent me a walking doll as big as a two years old. Oh, how I loved that doll, but she was taken from me never to be seen again. I cried so much but my doll was never seen again. A young child should have happy memories, not a heart full of tears.

Growing up in the country, I did not have any friends. My friends were my siblings and imaginary friends. I would give them names that I did not think existed, and then one day I found out that one of my imaginary friends name existed. I was shocked! My happy days were when my stepmother was not at home; my sisters would do my chores and watch me play. One day, I was told I had to change school. I sometimes asked myself why in the name of God did I have to change to a school farther away and I had to walk. There were no short cuts, So what was the purpose? I did not know anyone there. I was bound to be lonely. Maybe the reason was to feel lonely, I will never know. I had to "take it with a smile, remember you don't have a mother". Those were my father's words. He wanted me to take it with a smile.

My Mother Sleeps

CHAPTER 4
Portrait

Just before mama too ill, she had a photographer came to the house and took a portrait of the family. Her six children: Boyd the eldest boy, Valerie the eldest of the girls, Eucal, Heather, Massell, Eulice the baby, Papa, and herself. We all cherished that photo, not knowing at that time that would be the only thing we would have to keep us close to her. In the country in the early 1920 – 1944, no one in the poor countries had a camera. Everyday, I would look at that picture just to see my mama's face. That picture meant everything to me and the others, just to see her face every morning. Every time when I think how we were denied of that, it hurts even today. Tears come to my eyes. How cruel was that, but we had to take it with a smile. That kind of vindictiveness hurts. There is no words to express such ugliness. The only one out of the five of us at home was Eucal. Our stepmother, she had great plans for him. We would know it in the future. I remembered the Sunday my unsung hero, Boyd left home for the big city. I had cried so much seeing him with his little bag. "Where are you going?" I asked. "Don't cry, little one!" We were all crying. What would he be doing in the big city? We all tried to cheer each other up but we were missing him already.

My brother whenever I think of him, this poem of Henry Wadsworth Longfellow would come to mind. He Knew what he wanted out of life and he want after it. He owns his business, he was respected from one end of the island to the other.

In his death, people came from all over the country to pay their last respects.

The height of great men reached and kept
Were not attained by sudden flight.
But they, while their companions slept,
Were toiling upward through the night

           Henry Wadsworth Longfellow

Massel Smith

CHAPTER 5
BIG CITY

The years go by so fast and my life was changing just as fast. Few years after Boyd left we were told we were moving to the city. At first I was happy and excited. I will see Boyd everyday, I thought. But my excitement did not last for long. I started thinking my little sister, Eulice would be all alone. Who will she have to talk with? Who will she play with? As I am writing this, my tears are falling. I will have Heather, Valerie, and Eucal to talk with. But whom will she have? The great thing she has is love – love that I will never know, that I will never know. My sister, Eulice is the baby of my mother's children. We had great fun together even though we did not live in the same home. Then my eyes fill with tears once more. I was leaving my Mama. You see her grave was our connection. I would sit on her grave and talk with her. Now I am leaving for the big city. How will I talk with her? How will she know where to find me? I could not imagine but time would tell.

My Dad was not home often. He had to stay and see to the cows and the fields; I missed him not being home. Who would we talk with? Those time when we lived in the country, they were rough but we had our father with us. Now we hardly see him. He must be lonely for us as we are for him. My brother, Eucal was with him so we did not see him often. The family seems to be split up in a little pieces, but life still goes on. I was going to a new school. I did not know anyone there. I asked myself, "Is this what life is like in the big city?" Then out the blue, one day my Aunty came for me to live with her. My life now made a big turn. My Aunt that lived in America was planning to adopt me. They were preparing for me to go to America. It was different living with my Aunt. She lived the high society – type of life, I had to dress for dinner, I had clothes for the morning and for the evening. All her friends were rich and they lived the high society style. I was now going to a private school. At first, I felt I should not be there, I felt out of place; but that changed fast. I was now one of them and it felt good. No more will I be called (Crepe – sole) at my old school I wore white runners. They were always white as if they were coming straight from the store but

My Mother Sleeps

the sole was all eaten away. I would put cardboard inside the shoe so no one would know, for the uppers were lilly white. It is funny how life can change with the blink of the eye.

My stepmother did not like this; it was too good for me. So she said if I did not come home, my Aunt would have to take all of us. So, when I came home for the holidays, she did not let me go back. My dad did nothing about that; all for a quite life; Some quite life!

CHAPTER 6
MOTHER

Mother Dear Mother!

It is summer once more. As I sit here on this beautiful day, my thoughts turn to you

What would it be if you were here with me? What can I tell that you don't know?

If I say I am lonely without you, you might turn and say I miss you as well.

I try to picture your face to see your smile. I try to listen for your voice.

In my mind, I can hear the music in your voice. There is so much I want to share with you.

I would tell you all the great things. The joys growing up as well as sadness that comes with it.

Mother, dear Mother, there is so much I want to say.

Why did you leave me so soon?

Did you not know I would miss you?

Mother I needed you then and I could not find you. I needed you to wipe the tears from my eyes.

I needed you to kiss my finger to make it better. I missed you not being here when I could not find my way.

Mother, now I am a woman and I miss you even more. Mother, is Papa with you? I miss him very much. He would say to me, "If only your mother was here, she would be so pleased to see the woman you are." Papa tried to keep your image alive for us.

I LOVE YOU MOTHER.

MASSELL,

My Mother Sleeps

CHAPTER 7
IT WAS SATURDAY

It was a Saturday in July, the morning gave hope for a beautiful day.

The morning was calm; the sky was soft blue. But it was that morning that evil raised its huge head, engulfing me in its terror and erasing all thoughts of a lovely day. It was now hell on earth.

I still can hear that haunting voice screaming, "Get Out! Get Out!" Then I was bodily thrown out of the house, my home. I landed in the back garden. I was in a daze, what was happening to me? To us?

I felt the blow on each side of my face. The blood and tears were washing my face. This could not really be happening but the pain, blood, and tears were real. This scene was not from a horror movie, this was for real. I was now fearful. Where was I going to go? This beautiful morning, now full of sadness. Where would my sisters and I go? Heather and I were standing on the street in front of what used to be our home, no place to go, no breakfast, and our clothes were taken. Valerie was not at home, she was at the church.

Where was Papa? We needed him. He was back in the country, not knowing what was taking place with his children, We were defenseless.

As we stood there, Boyd our eldest came. He hugged us and wiped our tears.

How did he know we had no home anymore? We were like wanderers, no place to lay our heads I had never seen my brother so upset, our pain was his pain. Boyd tried to comfort us, I looked up the street and I could see Valerie coming. I ran to her. "What's going on?", She asked.

I was unable to say. I was crying so hard. Heather told her, now we were all crying. Then Valerie told us not to worry. She would go and see our Aunty Kathleen and she left. She did not take long. In a few hours, she was back with us. Aunty told her to go get us. We now had a place to lay our head. If I did not know before, I now know my Mother had a great friend in my Aunty Kathleen; she was always there when things were not right with us.

Massel Smith

My Aunt Kathleen opened her home and her heart to us. That is one debt we will never be able to repay.

As the evening turned to dusk, we sat at the dinner table. My Aunt said there was something she had to tell us. She said she knew something was not right with us, but could not think what it was. She went on to say in the morning as she was watering her garden, she felt the presence of our mother and she could not shake it off. As the day went on, she went and lay on her bed for a nap. She dreamt of out mother; she was sitting in a rocking chair at foot of the bed.

She said, "What is it Hilda?" Mama said to her "My children, my children. My poor children".

So she knew something was wrong with us. As I sat there listening to what Aunty had to say, I wished I was back in the country. I would sit on my Mother's grave and tell her make me whole and not so lost. I wiped the tears from my eyes and gave thanks for my Aunty Kathleen, may she ever be blessed.

My Mother Sleeps

CHAPTER 8
TERROR

By Massell Smith

Yonder lays the valley of tears.
Tears for love ones who will never be seem again.
Tears for the innocent child at play.
A life robbed!
Tears for the courageous stranger who's hope of glory; was smashed in the twinkle of an eye.
What hateful minds, could stoop so low?

And rob the world of joy.
There is silence all around.
A silence that sends shivers through you're veins.
The street now is painted in blood.
Bones and fragments lie in the chaos,
On the blood stained street.
A town! A country! In hysteric and fear.

Confused and scared, marked their faces.
What can you say to a child that asked?
What happened to daddy's feet and hands?
What makes such evil in man prevail?
Is life on this earth to be forever be smeared by hate.
My eyes are thirsty for my love ones.

Their love I can only hold in my heart;
Now they are gone forever.
Should I forever cry? For there is no peace to be found in this world.
Will my heart for every bleed for the innocence of a world that lost forever.

CHAPTER 9
LIFE IN A NEW WAY

My life now takes on a new turn. I am thankful for having an Aunty like Kathleen. I now have a roof over my head and food to eat. I did not have to wonder where I would sleep or what I would eat anymore. My Aunty Kathleen would make sure of that. May she always be blessed. Aunty Kathleen was no – nonsense person and I or we tried our best to please her and to make our lives happy. Aunty Kathleen's place was small and just right for one person. Now it was for four. We did not have bedroom but we had a cot. At nights, we would open in the hallway that's where we would sleep. It was not that comfortable but we had a home and we were thankful for it. We were happy and we made the best of our circumstances. No one could tell what life was like.

Aunty Kathleen did her best for us with what little she had and we were thankful. There is no word or words that can say or display our gratitude. Words will never be enough. Now when I think back on those days, this phrase come to mind. "When one door closes, another opens."

This door that had opened to me, to us has shaped our lives in such a wonderful way; in the knowledge we have gained, the teaching we have received and the respect that has shown to us has made us the women we are today. It was not easy but from little, came much. Today my sisters and I can walk through any door with our head held high. All the finer things in life, we had a taste of and no one can never take that away from me, from us.

My Mother Sleeps

CHAPTER 10
SCHOOL DAYS

School days! School days!

Oh, what wonderful days of learning. Washed away by the years, but in my mind, they will be remembered forever days when I can meet and make new friends, days when I look forward to plays, plays like Cinderella, Red Riding Hood these take place in grade one.

There were the Christmas and Easter pageants done every year, without them it would not be the same. At harvest time we would have an evening of musical concert by the choir.

Needless to say, I was in all of them, I love singing even if my notes are off.

Those were great days and I remembered them all twice a week we would go for nature walk and we would gather wild flowers and make necklaces and it was great fun to take part in sports. Also, to watch the boys. My brother, as well, playing football and cricket.

They would compete with others schools those were joyful days.

English Literature, History, Geography, Religious Knowledge and Math were my favorites.

I love to hear about distant place, I want to see them all, to see the world, all of it.

The Equator, the Tropic of Cancer, and Capricorn. I secretly vowed I would see them and more.

I did see them all and lots more. I remember standing at the Equator, mans' Imaginary line, one foot on the north side and one on the south.

I thought I would be hot but I needed a jacket. There is so much to see and learn in this life.

So many years have gone by, washed away by time but my memories will stay forever.

CHAPTER 11
COURAGE

Courage is that gut feeling in you. You can't stay in the rut of contentment. The door is locked, you can't get out. But you must; you can't stay there or you, or you will suffocate. It is like that drowning man that held on to a straw; if not he will drown. It is a reassurance of hope. The evening shadows were closing in on me. As I sat in the quite of the evening; I asked myself, "How did I get here?" My life's journey was written on a sheet that revealed every step of my way. It was all there for me to see. I know I should not look back; I should look ahead. Even if I will not be there in the future; I don't know what it holds for me. I have to have hope. For a child death is very traumatic. I have to remember "look not on yesterday if is gone; tomorrow may ever come." I have to have hope for tomorrow. It is hard for a young child not to see through and to understand, today I have mother and in a winkle of an eye when tomorrow comes she is gone never no more will she holds me in her arms or to hear her voice. Yesterday she sang for me, her voice will never know more be heard. The sleep of eternity takes over. When I was a small child, I would look at other children that had their mothers, I don't know if I envied them. I just thought that their lives were complete.

I missed the beauty of a mother, the bonding of mother and child. I long for the feel of her fingers through my hair. I missed that gentle – voice, telling me what I did was not acceptable. I missed the excitement seeing her walking up the little hill. I long to be able to throw my arms around her waist knowing I was safe, because she was at home.

What is it about a mother that makes you feel secure? I can only think of love. I am not just any one I am a part of her. How marvelous to be a part of love, and to know it. I feel there is nothing greater. I'll never know how it felt to have my mother kiss away my pain and fears making it better again; Oh, the innocence of a child! I remember how scared I was, but this gave me the strength I needed to give me the courage that would erase my fears. I asked myself; "what stands in the

My Mother Sleeps

way of courage?" FEAR, FEAR of the unknown. As I sat in the quiet of the evening I could not help thinking if only I had my mother, my life would be much better. I looked up to the heaven. The sky was blue, there were some white clouds floating across the sky. I cried out to my mother.

Mother! Dear Mother of mine.
Why did you leave me?
Far too soon you left your children.
Now I know you had to go.
The choice was not yours to make.
Your heavenly father wanted you home.
Mother dear Mother I love you.
  I will see you on the other side, where all our earthly sorrow will be washed away, and peace perfect peace will be ours forever.

Massel Smith

CHAPTER 12
RED DRESS

The child in the red dress
Looks up at the sky
Mama! Are you there?
Ho! Mama! Can you hear me?
A cotton ball cloud floats
Across the bright blue sky
The child cries out:
I can see you mama!
The moment is as still as the dead of the night.
The child listens for Mama's voice
But no words can be heard.
Mama's voice was silent
As the cotton cloud rolled by
A child's dream was lost
In the quite of the moment.

CHAPTER 13
NO PERFECT PERSON

No one in this world is perfect, try as you may, you will never find a perfect person and that is just that. My Aunty K, might believe that she was perfect but we knew that was not so. She was like all of us. We could not have people over without asking her first. I did not have any friends – only the people from church and school. She had rules that we had to live by. We tried our best to live up to them, that was ok with us. Valerie was no longer living with us; she was working and had her own little place. We did not see her often; sometimes on the weekend she would come to see us. She once said to us, "You just have to know when to move on". We were now living in bigger house. We had our own bedroom. The house was given by our Aunt that lived in the U.S., so we did not have to pay rent which was great. One evening, Aunty Kathleen asked me if I had a friend over to have lunch with me. Why was she asking me this? I could not fathom, she told me I could not have anyone over when she was not at home. So why this, I said no. She would not take no for an answer, I was telling the truth. I did not know what was going on with her, she just refused to take no, it was as if 'no' was not in her head – it was taking a break. The she slapped me and I would not say 'yes', not for all the tea in China. Then Heather came out of her room and took my hand and said "Aunty K! That is enough. You don't have a sister and you would not know what it is like, let her be." That did not sit well with her. She then said to me "you will have a roof over your head and if it is one potato, I will share but do not ask me for anything that is it." But she did not stop there. She went to say. "You are nothing." Even now my mind at times would take me back to those harsh words 'You will never amount to anything, you are a nobody'. Those words hurt to the very core of my being. I had to prove to myself that I am not nobody but somebody and it did matter who people see me as. Those terrible words hurt, but I know who I am. I am no longer at the bottom of the river. I have raised to the surface. Today those words, 'you are a nobody, you will never amount to anything'. I wiped the tears away because I know who I am and no one can make me feel less. Those words said in anger have been the instrument of my fight. They have given me the strength. They have kept me anchor to who I really am and the courage to move on.

It was coming to the end of summer and in two weeks, I should be back in school. I had worked all summer in a dentist's office. I did not know how much I was being paid; my pay was given to Aunty K. The dentist was a friend. I had a problem about how my school fees were going to be paid. I was very unhappy. Boyd helped but it would not be enough. Would I be going back to school? It looked as if I would not be going back. I did not know what to do. The only thing I know was to pray. So I went to the storeroom, closed the door, got down on my knees, and poured my heart out to the Lord. It was Thursday and I had choir practice. I was late; my eyes revealed I was crying. After choir Rev. MacNab asked me what was wrong. So I told him what was going on with me. He prayed with me and told me not to worry. Everything would turn out just right, you will see. He then drove me home. On Friday, there was a knock on the gate and the dogs were making a great deal of noise. I went to see who was at the gate – it was Rev. MacNab. He asked for my school books. I got them together and gave them to him and he left. He did not tell me why he wanted my books. I did not ask but I was puzzled. On Wednesday of the following week at Youth Fellowship, Rev. MacNab told me I have to see Mrs. Clarke. She is the Rector's wife and the head mistress of one of the three Top High School for the girls in the country. I could not believe what I was hearing; I was shaking as a leaf in the wind. I went to see Mrs. Clarke at 5 PM. She told me I was going to start school at Queens on Monday. I could not believe what I was hearing. Me – Massell, was going to go to Queens. Was this real? Am I dreaming? Me, going to Queens? Touch me! Wake me up! I open my mouth to speak but no sound could be heard. I was truly blown away with the news. My cheeks were wet. I tasted the salt of my tears on my lips. I could not find any words to say except thanks and more thanks.

My Mother Sleeps

CHAPTER 14
QUEENS HIGH SCHOOL

Queens High School, one of the three top high schools for the girls in the country. This was a school where the children of the rich and famous attend. Now I am going I am going there too. I never thought that I would be rubbing shoulders with them. Never in my widest dreams could I see this happening. If this is a dream, don't wake me up. But this was not a dream, this was real. I am wide awake. I, who at one time did not have a place to lay my head, would be attending Queens High School. Now, I do not see my glass half empty but half full. Every morning, I get dressed in my uniform, my gray tunic, white blouse, black shoes, white socks and red beret with its logo on it. I was now living my dreams. I have found my glass slippers so I would go back to that Thursday in Mrs. Clarke office when she said to me, "I have looked at your work, quite impressive. You will be starting at Queens on Monday morning." This keeps me humble and thankful. A debt I will never be able to pay. My heart is over flowing with gratitude. Life never stays the same it is always moving day by day and I have learned to move with it. In the demise of happiness, there can be sadness mixed with joy. Now Heather would be living soon for Canada for good. She had a job waiting for her, so she did not mind Aunty Kathleen telling her to go. She would get some quality time with Valerie. But what would become of me? For sure the time would come when Aunty Kathleen would ask me to go.

So, Heather and I planned after school that, I would wait for her at Shirley's home, one of our church friend. That morning when I was leaving for school, it was very hard. I could not tell Aunty Kathleen this was the last time I would be saying goodbye to her as I leave for school. I just could not tell Aunty Kathleen that I was leaving too. In her mind, she should be the one telling me to leave; not me telling her. I had written her a letter telling her how grateful I am to her, and I will never be able to show her, not in a lifetime, how grateful I am. Then as I kept writing., my thought go back these words "You are nobody you will never amount to anything". Words said in anger hurt to the last bone in your body. This is life.

CHAPTER 15
TEENAGE YEARS

Teenage years are the hardest time for most. You never know if you are coming or going. You just have to move with it, ready or not. Time never stands still nor will wait for you. And, if you fall; you have to pick yourself up; dust yourself off; and go on. There will be lots of falls to come. Remember it takes you where you want to go, and you have to decide where you want to go. That is the joy of being young.

It is quite funny that when I left Aunty Kathleen that morning, on my way out of the door my heart was crying. It seems that I can't get myself to forget that morning. I was hoping she would have understood why things turned out the way. I always remember what Valerie said to Heather and me sometime ago: "The time will come when you will know that it is time to go." At this present time, she will not have anything to do with me. Well, that's life. I just have to face it and move on. I must make sure that this gift that was given to me is the passport to my future. I have to make sure that my school work would always come first. My life now will turn to what will I do after high school. I love teaching. I remember as a kid I would play with my imaginary friends. I used the subs that mixed in the rose garden as the kids and I was the teacher. I was happy with my pretending to be a teacher, so that is what I will be. Now that I have decided what I will be, I must now work to bring it to fulfillment.

This was the last year in high school and I was going to start a job at the Ministry of Education on Monday. It was for six month and I loved it. It was the beginning of my new life. After the six month, I got a job as a manager of a boutique that was mainly for tourists. This was great! I had the pleasure of meeting people from all over the world and different walks of life. These tourist come from places that I studied in History and Geography, places that I hope one day I would visit in the future. This job was great I had enjoyed it beyond words. This is not what I wanted to do for the rest of my life. I had my dreams and I should follow them and make them come to reality. I loved what I am doing now but something was missing. I had to find the missing piece.

On Tuesday evening as I walked through the door, Valerie gave me a letter. This letter was from the Director of an upscale Prep School and when I say upscale – I mean just that. The parents were the top of the crop – upscale politicians, prime minister, diplomats, and judges… the list goes on. She wanted me to come in for an interview and meet the other board members. Can you imagine how I felt? Just boiling over with excitement. Monday was too far away.

I must say the interview went well, I felt great. Then on the Tuesday, I got a call from the Headmistress. I had the job. It was one of the happiest days of my life. My dream has to come to life. It is wonderful feeling to work with kids. They are so eager to learn and they say the darnest things. They are inquisitive and interesting. They showed no fear when it comes to learning. I remember one morning this little boy was going to give me gift. As he saw me, he started running to me, calling out, "Miss Smith, Miss Smith. I have a gift for you. It is a secret, bubble bath." I just had to smile. Kids – they are so spontaneous. On Saturdays I worked in a department store as a supervisor. Now when I look back on those days it gives me a lift and put a smile on my face.

CHAPTER 16
LIVING WITH SISTER VALERIE

Living with my sister Valerie was far less stressful than with Aunty Kathleen. Aunty Kathleen had so many rules to follow. There is nothing wrong with rules, but sometimes the rule maker goes overboard. My Aunty Kathleen was just like that. What she says, goes. With her, you have to make sure you mind your Ps and Qs. Make sure you cross your t and dot your i, there is no room for mistakes. Saying all of this helps shape me in to who I am today. I had the bitter and the sweet.

As young miss, I was very shy. In the house across the street were some young men from Panama. They were studying at the University. The youngest of the group was living in Jamaica for some time. He was in love with my sister, Eulice. In the evening, they would come over to our house and we would play cards. The youngest of the group, Delano told his brother, Tony about me and gave him my address. So we became pen pals. He was a very gentle spirit. A great friendship developed between us. I could tell him everything that was going on in my life and he would understand and guide me through what I had to do. No matter what it was he would help me find the answer.

It was great to receive his letters every day of the week but mostly Fridays. I would look forward to his letters it was fun to read them. I had to read them through the mirror. His letters were for my eyes only.

He opened my eyes to so much I did not know about growing up. He was in a different country, but at times it was as if he was right beside me holding my hands. He will forever be in my heart as long as I live. When I look back on those days of having Tony as a friend, I felt blessed although we were apart. He has a part of my heart that not even time can erase. His letters were special gift that I will keep forever, they were part of who he is.

There are two young men – Neville and Chester, that have taking a great part of my life. We were always together and I was happy. These

Massel Smith

men cared for me and they respected me. Then one day Neville left for Canada. Once, there were three; now there are two.

Chester and I became closer in many ways. Life was kind to me, I felt I was loved. In life, things do not always remain the same. There are times when things change without you realizing it. They can take your happiness and tear it to pieces.

My Mother Sleeps

CHAPTER 17
LEAVING MY LAND OF BIRTH

The day finally came when I was leaving this land of my birth to a land I hardly knew. My heart was beating so fast. I was excited and I was scared. It is one thing to visit and another to take the country as your home. A million different thoughts and questions were going on in my head. I was sad and yet I was excited. It is too late to turn back now. The plane circled around the city before it really took off. I sat there with my eyes glued to the window. The city looked so tiny like a drop in the sea. As the plane rose higher and higher, I was now caught between the glorious blue sky and the lily white clouds just like the first falling of snow. It looked so peaceful. It was as if I was coming out of a dream. I have made my choice I must see it through. Will this Canada be my new home? As I sat there wondering if this country will be good to me; I could not help but think of the country I am leaving. It has been my home from the day I was born. This tiny island has stood so many trials and tribulations. I started thinking from whence it came to be.

Jamaica! Jamaica! A paradise in the sun; surround by the blue Caribbean Sea.
So small, yet so big through the hearts of your people.
You stand 4,244 square miles, smaller then Connecticut.
Yet you are the fifth largest Island of the Caribbean.
Lying 90 miles south of Cuba, 100 miles west of Haiti.
Your coastal lowland is a limestone plateau.
In the East a group of volcanic hills the great
Blue Mountains – stand.
You were the first home of the peaceful Arawak Indians.
Your people have always struggled to be on their own.
Yet with all your on – tap wealth, you were never your own.
You were the possession of Spain in 1494.
The British flag stood proudly claiming its possession in 1655.
Your shores are know stranger to disasters.
When disaster raised its ugly head, our pain is felt by everyone.

Massel Smith

Port Royal stands as proof to tell the story of the earthquake of June 7, 1692;
When the sea claimed it for a short time.
Now it stands on its own, away from Kingston
The story of Port Royal teaches it own lesson.
It was once the capital of this island in the sun.
The wealthiest and wickedest city in the world, ruled by the pirates and the buccaneers.
This came to an end on June 7, 1692.
Yet to this day there is a belief that the spirits of Henry Morgan and his fellow buccaneers remain inhabitants of this once bustling town.
The time was a hand for you to think of your future.
I will break from your mighty grip.
I will say to the powers that be "My freedom is mine. So now I will rule my people"
Oh motherland!
I can still remember – the cool breeze and the bright sun, upon my face.
This day is to be treasured.
You have come of age.
On August 6, 1962 you are now free and part of the Commonwealth. Your Governor – General, he is the Queen's representative appointed by her. Your head of State is the Prime Minister elected by the people. I can hear the music of your drums, as your people sway to its beat.

Beautiful land, you are a country of many races Chinese, Indians, Irish, and Scottish. In 1660 you became a refuge for the Jews in the New World.

Oh, Jewel of the Caribbean the world knows you for the Bauxite, Sugar Cane, Banana, Blue Mountain Coffee, Rum and the Red Stripe Beer.

On the international stage you have done well. In track and field, the athlete, Usain Bolt, became the fastest man.

In cricket you are well known. For a country that does not have snow, you sent a bobsled team to the Winter Olympics as seen in the movie, Cool Running's.

My Mother Sleeps

CHAPTER 18
MONTREAL

Montreal is great city but it can also be a lonely one if you are far away from home and all alone. I miss my sisters and my brothers but if you want your dreams to come to light, at times you have to go through the thorns before you get to the clearing now, I was going through the thorns and a times they hurt. I am feeling the pain now but the time will come when I will smile, for if not all for sure some of my dreams will be fulfilled.

I remember I sat on my bed and I was crying. I was very lonely, I was alone. The dog came to my room and rested its head on my lap and was making sounds as if to say don't cry you are not alone. I then wiped my eyes then my thoughts went back to my childhood. Aunt Kathleen was a nurse and at times she would have to work at nights., So when she left for work, the dogs would take up their guards. One would be between the bedrooms; one would be at the backdoor and one would be at the front door. They were taking care of me; I rubbed is head and said thanks. I would always laugh at this, they were standing guard for us.

Living in Montreal and not knowing the language was a trying time. I remember one day, I was going to a place for the first time, I asked the bus driver For help he said to me "I do not speak English". This was at the time English speaking people were leaving Montreal, it was a bad time. I remember my friends Neville and Chester came to Montreal to see me. We were going to a function. We were not sure so we asked this young man for help, he said to us, "I am sorry but I do not speak English." We looked at each other and had a good laugh. I have learned never to underestimate the powers of God. He never fails. When bad things happen in my life, my first thought is to reach out to the Heavenly Father.

Try me, oh God and know my thoughts; see if there be any wicked ways in me.

I have learned as a small child that the Divine Creator loves me more than even me loving me.

He has said; "As I have been with Moses so shall I be with you. I will never leave you nor for sake you."

These are powerful words from my Heavenly Father.

My Mother Sleeps

CHAPTER 19
THE GROWTH OF A WOMAN

SEVENTY – THREE YEARD

Life! Oh Life! Like the flame of a candle your strength comes from a higher power that lies within.

Just like the light of a candle, surrounded by glass that finds its strength at the base which flickers and shimmy to its peak.

With a sense of grace, of confidence, you rise to the top. Know how much to ask of yourself and how much to give.

You have touched many with your openness and generous heart letting your inner beauty shine through.

Where! Oh Where! Have the years gone? Just yesterday you had pigtails and bright colour ribbons.

Today you stand like a fortress full of courage and wisdom.

Seventy years have taught you well.

There is gentleness, warmth and assurance that beams through you, giving whoever that comes within its rays.

Confidence and a new way to see life.

A light that will never die

You have lived seventy – three years upon this earth, living dreams you have so dearly you have tasted the bitter and savored the sweet fruit of life.

Overcome adversity, heartache and strife. One thing you know, your happiness begins and ends with you.

Massel Smith

CHAPTER 20
BROKEN WINGS

THE APHASIA INSTITUTE AND PAT ARATO CENTRE

What it has done for me.
I know a place which is the Aphasia Institute and Pat Arato Center.
A brain tumor as its way to make one feel helpless and lost.
After surgery to remove the tumor, my life took on a new phase.
I had never heard of the word Aphasia before, but I would soon find out
I was lost within myself.

But I would soon find a place that would let me see my glass half full.
This place the Aphasia Institute was recommended to me by my speech
Language Pathologist, "The Aphasia Institute and the Pat Arato Centre".
Oh what a place; it took me from darkness and into the light. What a blessing I came to the Center with broken wings and it as showed me that I can still fly.

CHAPTER 21
TIME TO MOVE ON

The time had come for me to move on. I had a decision to make. Should I go to New York or Toronto? In New York, I have my fairy godmother, my aunt Dinie and a very good friend Precious and her three girls. We are friends from back in Jamaica. So with all this I decided on New York.

I was able to see my aunt every day. We were two houses apart.

I took a course in PN. When that was over. I got job in that field. Precious was also a nurse and at times she had to work nights so I was there for the girls. Precious was outgoing. She had many friends. She introduced me to one of her friends, a very handsome young man. We had a lots in common. He was a gentleman and he loved me very much. He would never go to sleep before he called, even if he just left me. He just had to say; "Good night little Indian." Even when I moved to Toronto, he would make sure he called me every night. I was very broken up when we had to say goodbye. At one time, he was going to move to Toronto so we could be together; but that is life, you win some and you lose some. I remember once when he came to see me here in Toronto. He was very gentle and when he was with me he would do everything for me. My sister, Eulice once said to me, "He loves you so much," I said to her, "But he has not asked me to be his wife." Sometimes I think this is my lot in life. I get very sad at times and this sadness can eat at your very core. I know I have to pick myself up and dust myself off and get on with my life. This at times eats away at your strength. My loneliness was doing just that to me. No one knew just how much I hurt.

I hide behind my smile but when I am alone and I closed the door, the river overflows its banks and life goes sadly on.

CHAPTER 22
LEAVING NEW YORK

Leaving New York was one of my saddest days. I am now in Toronto I have no friends here in Toronto. Even though I have my sisters, it was a lonely time for me. I have to find a job. I had registered with manpower. This is a government agency. My experience with finding a job was something quite strange. There were jobs around but there was always someone ahead of me.

The last time I was at the agency Mr. Andrew saw a job advertisement. I was sitting in his office when he made the call. Mr. Mark Jones told him to send me over. I was only five minutes from his office. I got there and asked to speak with Mr. Mark Jones only to be told he was not in. I was a bit perplexed, so I said "Mr. Andrew just spoke with him and he was expecting me, "Well he is not here. He will call you in the evening at your home." So, I gave him my phone number, thanked him, and left.

I had a strange feeling that Mr. Mark Jones would not call me. I could see through his story. I thought, "How can a person act like that?" That I will never know. I did not expect him to call, and he never did. That was my first time of facing racism. I though how sad, but I was not going to give up. I have to eat and find a place to live. I was determined.

On my way home as I passed the Riverdale Hospital, I got off the bus and went in to the hospital to see if there was any vacancy. Everything was strange to me, but that did not stop me. There, I was told they would get in touch with me later in the week. I felt confident that I would have a job.

There was a nursing home not far from where I was staying. So instead of going home. I went there to see if there were any available jobs. At the office I asked to speak with the Nursing Director. I was told she could not see me. I had no appointment and that there was opening.

My Mother Sleeps

I then asked to speak with the person in charge of Housekeeping Department. By this time, I was getting the clear picture. So, I asked to speak with the person in charge of the kitchen. I was determined to push a little further. So, I said could I have an application. She looked me up and down and then grudgingly and gave me the application.

CHAPTER 23
THE DECISION

I filled out the application to the Director of Nursing and gave it to her. I had written her name down from the identification on her desk, thanked her, and left. I had this feeling she knew I was not going to take her word that there was no opening.

As I walk up the street, I could see Heather on the balcony waving frantically at me. She was trying to tell me something but I was not getting all of it. As I got to the door, she met me telling me I had to go back to the Nursing Home. The Director wants to talk with me. So of course, I went back. I got the job and I was to start right away. I was so happy. Two days after I got the job at the hospital, my joy was overflowing.

In that same week I got my apartment at the building next to Heather. My sister, Eulice was going to live with me.

I now have two jobs – one in the morning and the other in the evening. That was not all, I have an apartment. I was so happy I had to pinch myself to make sure I am awake. When I look back on sees you different from him or herself? Your colour lies on the outside, but what is in the inside is what counts.

My Mother Sleeps

CHAPTER 24
TWO JOBS

I have two jobs and my apartment. I have settled quite well in Toronto. I have started to see some of my dreams come to life. I made my first trip by myself away from Canada to Bahamas. This trip was great. I met a lovely young man, Brian. I had a fabulous time. Every night was great as long has Brian was around. I was quite comfortable with him. He took me all over the Island. One day, I met Cherry from Oshawa. Sometimes we would hangout together. One day Brian took me out fishing. Cherry came along and Brian invited a friend. Oh what a great time I had! This was my first time, what exciting time that was! The excitement was not just about fishing. We were fishing in the Atlantic Ocean where the Caribbean Sea joins the Atlantic Ocean. That was just great fun. I caught a fish. What excitement that was! I could not bring the fish in. It was so big. I was shouting for help full of excitement. We had that fish for dinner. What a day that was. I can honestly say, that was the highlight of my trip. Nice people, good wine, and plenty of sun.

My second trip was a cruise from Montreal to Florida. When I got to Montreal, I remembered seeing three girls. They were looking at me but they did not speak nor did I. That first night at dinner. They were sitting a few tables away from me. They kept watching me and saying something about me – good or bad. You just feel it by their actions. Their eyes seem to go right through you. Well, the next night at dinner I did not see them at the table. I said to myself "Oh they went to the early sitting." As I was about to sit the head waiter came to me and said there is someone who would like you to join them. I was taking aback but I went. I was not surprised to see the three girls, so I sat down. They introduced themselves as Pat, Loraine and Dorothy I introduced myself. They are Americans, then Pat said that they wanted me to sit with them but I looked so proud with my head held high. They thought that I would not sit with them. I told them that I am sure I am not like that. They are mistaking me for someone else. They all started laughing so hard I joined them we had a great laugh together. That was how great friendship was born. They too want to see the world. We had great times together. We took lots of trips together. I was so happy to have met them that I would not have to travel alone. We all want to see the world in all of its glory. What more could one ask for? We all have so much in common. The Americans – Pat, Loraine and Dorothy, we share each other joys, laughter and tears. They are great to be with.

My Mother Sleeps

CHAPTER 25
ONE NEVER KNOWS

One never knows where life will take you; one just has to brace his – self or her – self to be strong; and not to give in without a try. If you give up, who will hold your hand? I never asked to be here on this earth, but I am here.

I don't know what tomorrow will bring, but I know I have to be here. My sisters stayed with me the night before the surgery so they could accompany me to the hospital. I had to be there for five a.m. Needless to say I did not sleep a wink; my thoughts would not let me. I dreaded the morning. Would I be laughing at the end of the day? That was something I had to wait to find out.

When it was time for me to go to the operating theatre, a very tall and huge orderly came to escort me. My sisters were not allowed to accompany me. As I walked with him, he adjusted his steps so I could keep up with him.

As I walked this endless corridor, I could hear a bird chirping. I felt lost and alone. I thought, "This must be how one feels when taking their last walk," lost and alone. I looked outside and I could see the frost on the grass as the early morning sun did its magic. My heart refused to acknowledge it.

I asked myself, "Will I ever see the sunshine again?" The tears were in my eyes. I was fighting to keep them there. As I walked beside this orderly, I appeared composed, but in truth I was scared, frightened and alone.

I went into the pre – op room and I was cold as ice and shaking like a leaf in the wind. Two toasty warm blankets were covering me, but I was still cold. I could see my sisters and my niece standing at the door just looking in on me Dr. B. told them to come in. They told me not to worry. Right there and then the words of Dr. B. came back to me, when I said to him, "My life is in your hands." He turned and said this: "I will do my best, but when you are dealing with the brain anything can happen."

Those words are always with me. If I did not know what they meant then, I sure know now Dr. B. let my family stay until the door of the theater closed and they could not see me anymore.

Life changes for everyone. Our past molds the future and our present shapes it. I say this with sincerity. As I look back on my life, I ask myself, "How did I get where I am today?" I draw strength from my yesterdays. My tomorrows are not promised to me. So, I lived in the now. As I lie here, my thoughts go back to the day in the chief anaesthetist's office. He was telling me about the different kinds of anaesthesia. I turned to him and said, "Are you going to put me to sleep?" He paused for just a moment. The expression on his face was priceless, and then he said; "Lady! It is not a worth we are removing from your finger!" As I lied there, I thought, "What a silly question."

As they put me on the operating table, I was so cold, worried and scared. I was praying, then the doctor said, "Think happy thoughts." That was the last thing I remembered. I was awakened to a gentle voice calling my name – "Massell." Then I would drift off once more. I had no idea how long I was drifting in and out of sleep, but I knew each time she called my name and I opened my eyes I would see an angel sitting at the foot of my bed. That gave me great comfort and a sense of peace. The last time she called my name I could see the angel sitting at the foot of my bed was my nurse.

After I left the hospital I was under the care of a neurologist. It took one year to realized that I had aphasia. I remembered I was in the neurologist's office and I was repeating over and over the same thing: "When am I going back to work?" Which I did not know I was doing. She said "Enough! Enough Now!" In a strong voice. I told my sisters and all the people I moved with that if I kept on repeating my name please stop me. I could not tell anyone who I am. I would take out my driver's license to show them.

My Mother Sleeps

My neurologist sent me to rehab, which was where I learned of aphasia. My speech – pathologist referred me to the Aphasia Institute. That is where I learned the true meaning of the word aphasia.

Massel Smith

CHAPTER 26
Dear Massell,

The years go by so fast. Only yesterday I was twenty, today I am seventy – three.

Where have those years gone? I see them as a big race. If I knew what I know now, would that have made a difference? I will never know.

Experience comes from learning and time waits for no one. To make dreams come true you have to live your dreams.

Put yourself in those dreams. Take the bull by the horns.

Sometimes a little selfishness does no harm. Think of yourself first.

Time passes and will never come back.

As I sit here in the twilight hour, with the gentle breeze brushing my cheeks.

Would it have made a difference? I will never know if I had taken what was mine.

Time teaches wisdom and understanding. Today I am glad I let time run its race.

My regrets are small; my joys have out – numbered them. When I look back on my days living with my aunty Kathleen, I remember the day she told me 'I was a nobody and I would not amount to anyone'.

Today, no tears come to my eyes. That chapter is long time closed and I can lift my head high and I know that no one could ever make me feel that small ever again.

Those words that was uttered to me in anger have been my strength and courage to achieve my dreams and to move forwards, I realize when something is said in anger – no matter what, use it in a way that makes the good in you shine throughout your life.

I know this for sure: If Aunty Kathleen was alive, she would be proud of me.
Massell Smith.

CHAPTER 27
THE JOY OF LIVING

To be alive is to feel the gentle breeze in your hair.
To see the humming bird dancing around the apple blossom.
To hear the cries of a new born baby.
To feel a mother's arms around you.
To be alive is to wake up each morning with the sun shining through the window.
To be alive is to enjoy the simple things of life.
Being alive is to love yourself and others, we are all part of the master's creation
Being alive is to treat others as you would want to be treated.
The simple things of life are free.
To see the brook slowly, moving down stream.
Hear the movement of the water as it hits the rocks that are in its way, as it makes its way lazily down stream.

CHAPTER 28
THE THINGS WE FACE IN LIFE

The things we face in life are sometimes tragic, but out of that tragedy comes strength. One thing I know for sure life does not just stop, because something is broken. You fix it the best way you can and move on. My tears will not let it go away. Yet I know I have to let go as difficult as it is. I must find a way.

Now my surgery was over but did my life return to the way it was before. I can surely say no, I was constantly crying. I could not figure what was going on. My whole life was upside down. I could not understand why my life was in such a mess.

My life now was just like my childhood, when I would cry about everything for nothing. My dad was my security blanket. He was the last one at night and the first one in the morning. I believe it was because I had lost my mother at such a young age.

In the early years after my surgery I had lost all my confidence and my self-esteem. I could not even make the simplest of decisions. I found myself having to learn all over again. The flood gates were once more opened, I am now a weeping Willow. But I have to say out of the sorrow comes great joy.

My like took on a course I did not know. I just could not figure out what was going on. After I came to terms with myself, I started to rebuild my life. I started see things in a new light.

At first in my life, a life that I am now living, I have to say acceptance was the key. I now know what my neurosurgeon meant when he said to me, "When you are dealing with the brain anything can happen." I know what that anything is. I have Aphasia. This is a disability with no face. So, at first when you meet someone it is hard for that person to comprehend what you are facing. Aphasia is a communication disability, not just talking but understanding well.

My Mother Sleeps

CHAPTER 29
BE AWAKE

*This is the time to awake from slumber and spread joy to all.
This is a time when life is moving around us
A time when rivers, brooks, springs and lakes are alive once more.
The trees that had shed leaves are now alive and in full bloom.
What joy is given to us human, joy unspeakable
To see this miracle of life around us.*

To hear the birds singing in the trees as they perched on there naked branches.

Squirrels are out of their hiding and enjoying the beauty of spring.

At first in my new life, a life that I am now living, I have to say acceptance is the key.

I now know what my neuro – surgeon meant when he said to me, "When you are dealing with the brain anything can happen", I now have aphasia. This disability as no face.

It is a communication disability. Not just taking but understanding as well.

One thing I know for sure, life does not just stop it goes on. Even the tinniest mustard seed if nurtured will grow.

In this new life of mine I see spring in a new way.

Before spring was just another season. I miss the beauty of it. Now I see every shade of green.

This I did not see before.

There is a significant force in my life that shines through the darkness of my life,

That keeps me grounded in the blessings of life.

Massel Smith

CHAPTER 30
BONDED BY BIRTH

Sister! dear sister of mine.
How can my heart show and tell of
The love it feels.
Though being older I have known you all
My life, and you me.
At times you have been my mother and
Times you have been my friend.
You have protected and shielded me
When I needed it most.

Precious sister of mine
The road you have traveled
Has been long,
tedious and tiring.
The mountains were high and steep
Valleys deep and treacherous
But there were still many cool shades
Along the way with rivers to
Quench your thirst.
And the creator shows his great
Love for you

Those beautiful hazel eyes once
Sparkled with life
Now sadden, cloudy with pain and tiredness.
Has I watched her sleep I bit my lips
To still the hurt.
So little, few, youthful carefree days spent.
Too many tears were shade and
A brave hearth fight back.

My Mother Sleeps

So peaceful you rest
While my thoughts rush on
Your faith in our creator is the glue
That kept you strong.
I try to hide the tears that flow
How can I, my heart is breaking so.
Like a mother to me you were.
When wrongly accused, harshly scold
 You took my hand in yours
Leading me away you had words so strong
But gently spoken from a child to an adult
Words that tell of pain and the love you felt.
"Enough! Let her be!
You never had a sister; You don't know what it is
Like to have a sister."
When it was time to leave your nest
You took me with you.
   Like a soldier you stand ready for the duty call
Giving much of yourself
Getting very little in return
So easily misunderstood by many
At times you seem so distant to others
But only a shield to protect yourself from hurt
So like an oyster that precious, delicate,
Beautiful; gem is hidden inside.

I am so blessed Oh Sister! For having you
I love   you and thank you for all
You have brought to my life
You may not be an angel But truly are a Saint
It is only through the eyes of Love and Bonding
The oyster will reveal the exquisite pearl inside

I Love You Sweet Sister Of mine.

Precious Sister of mine the road you have traveled
Has been long, tedious and tiring.

Massel Smith

The mountains were high and steep.
Valleys deep and treacherous.
But there were still many cool shades,
Along the way, with rivers to
Quench your thirst.
And the creator shows his great love for you.

Sister dear! You have let me on your joys.
And I have weathered many storms
With you.
Now the storm you face, is bigger than you and I.

How bravely you
in anguish as I watched in horror the
Struggles you face

My Mother Sleeps

CHAPTER 31
LIFE HAS CHEATED ME

*Oh where has yesterday gone?
Was I to be blamed, for what I did or did not do.*

*I was too young to see and understand it all.
As a very tinny child I remember one day my beloved mother was taken from me, to a place where
I could not go. I did not fully understand what death was all about. What I did know was Mama was
Put in a box then the lid of the box was closed. I could no longer see her face. For at three years how
Could anyone tell me I would never no longer see my Mama's face. For a three years old how could any-one tell Me I would not see my Mama every again.
Could anyone prepare me for a life without a mother. A mother is the stable part of a child's life and upbringing.
A mother gives love and shows love to her children. She nurtures, correct them she is there to watch over her infants and wiped their tears. She kisses the cut on the finger to make it better.
She tells stories she made up as if they were true. She takes them the first day to school and when they
Return she is there to greet them with open arms. What is there that makes a mother so special.
It is that understanding, unselfish love, love that can only be see in a mother.
Where was my mother at that time in my life? I needed her then, but death had taken her away far too
Soon. What a cruel blow it delivers!
For a mother's love is this, love that knows no boundaries. It is love that radiate through every fiber
Of her body. A love that is not selfish. A love that can not be bought. A mother's love teaches to be
Humble, see only the good in all of us.
A mother's love crosses all boundaries and that is what life cheat's*

Massel Smith

me of.
   What is that love a baby clink to.
   What is that smile a baby see that makes the eyes shine bright and the gentle arms incircle her.
   The kiss that so softly place upon the cheeks.
   Those are the loving things a mother does for her children

CHAPTER 32
THE SILHOUETTE ON THE HILL

The meadow was wide.
The meadow was green
Wildflowers everywhere
The silhouette of a figure
Could be seen on the hill

The figure just stood there
Oblivious to all around
The figure was looking
Across the sea where the sea
And sky blend as one

There were joyful sounds
Of the birds in the tree
A lark way up high in a crab- apple
Tree, overseeing the land,
Calls her babies to come on home
The ground doves were cooing as
They walked around this figure
The butterflies and bees were buzzing
Every where.
As the breeze was blowing gently.
The air was filled with the aroma
Of wildflowers.
There was a hint of salt in the air
Yet this figure seems not to move

Was it I who stood on that hill?
I who have eyes but fail to see
The majestic beauty of the sea
And sky blend as one.

Massel Smith

Was it I who have ears to hear
The music of the birds, and
the sweet
Calling of the lark. and the cooing
Of the dove.

Was it I who can feel, yet did not felt
The soft gentle wind on my cheeks.
Was life that hard or cruel.
And robs me of this too.
Was it I who have lips
That never tasted the salt in the air
Was it I who have the sense of smell
And even so not smell and enjoy
The essence of the air.
Was it I whose pain, hurt and loneliness
Blind me of all of this
Or was it you

CHAPTER 33
MY THREE WISHES

Life's journey has taken me far and wide and I have learned how to be thankful.

If I had my life to live over I would make sure my mistakes were not the same.

This is what I would give myself: Three Wishes,

My first wish would be to see my mother. I do not know my mother - she died when I was three.

Can a child remember at such young age?

My second wish would be to fulfill my dream and see the world – all of it.

I have seen a lot but there is lots more to be seen.

I have learned a lot from these journeys.

My third wish would be to see life more clearly.

To appreciate my life in so many ways.

To be thankful for what I have today. Yesterday is gone, but I have today; I have come a long way.

My blessing are many and I am thankful for today.

Yesterday is gone, and tomorrow my never be.

When life's burdens engulf me and dark clouds surround me,

There is a Father who will carry me through.

Massel Smith

CHAPTER 34
DINNER WITH MAMA

My greatest joy would be to have dinner with my Mama.
I can picture her sitting across the table, telling me how to use my knife and fork.
I could see her smiling face across the table.
She would cook what I like.
I am a picky eater, she would promise me something special if I eat all my dinner
Telling me not to use my fingers to pick up my food.
This was not done at the table.
"Mama, I went swimming today in Uncle's river."
Mama looks up: "I told you kids not to go swimming."
No one lifts their head.
My brother would say, "what did you do today Mama?"
Mama would smile and say,
"Well, I made you children dinner.
She would not tell she was making our Easter clothes.

My Mother Sleeps

CHAPTER 35
THOUGHTS ON FRIENDSHIP

I was sitting by the window just gazing outside, the evening was quiet and peaceful.

Through the window I could see a lonely figure standing there just gazing at setting sun.

She seems so lost and lonely, beaten by a world of cares and betrayals. No one to talk with, no one cares. I saw a figure retreating within herself, as a pearl within an oyster.

What makes the pain so hard to bear? Hurt by a friendship that was never there.

I strolled outside in a field of grass; blades so tall we became as one.

The magic of the setting sun warm upon my face. I started to ponder the true meaning of friendship. What should I look for? Is it to be pain and deceit? I through of the figure gazing at the sun set. How could friendship be so cruel to one that was trusting? As I reflect upon the word, I soon found out what true friendship should be.

Is it the hand that reached out and got burned?
No! it is that hand that so firmly held, implying you are not alone.
Is it those bitter words so harshly spoken?
No! it is those gentle words spoken in love. That say I understand.
Is it the love that is given in deceit?

As I walked along, I asked the question of myself. What really is friendship?
Is it harmony of sharing oneself?
It is trusting. The foundation of friendship.
True friendship is not deceitful.
True friendship breaks no trust.
True friendship is accepting the other as he or she truly is with all their strong and weak points.
Friendship is like fresh rain on your face.
That is the joy and blessing of having a friend.

CHAPTER 36
TO BE STRONG

Life journey is not very easy road.
One's strength is for every tested
My strength lives within me which make me strong
My life is forever presented with new challenges that demands all my strength.
Dark clouds overshadow the light in my life
Light that I need to go forward.

Where will I find the strength? To show that I can be strong, that is bigger than me.
I believe in a greater power
This power will always keep me centered.
There is always hope for a brighter tomorrow.
Without that hope I will never make it.

Mother Nature is always teaching me from the rising of the sun to the going down of the same.
This teaches me that beauty can also be ugly that white virgin snow as its black side.
Dry grass can become green once more,
After a shower of rain.

CHAPTER 37
THE MAN WITH THE GOLDEN VOICE

When he sings his voice gives new meanings to the words
It opens the mind to see and hear clearly the full harmony and the rebirth of each word,
Leaving you entrapped within each verse.
A new song has born from the depth of old words
His voice reflects who he really is;
He always have a smile
For everyone and a second to say hello.
His heart is touched by each member's story
He has seen how to vulnerable each member is.
Just as the Aphasia logo whispers you are not alone.
Tonight, in many ways we the members are saying through
This concert and THE MAN WITH THE GOLDEN VOICE:
We are surely not alone.

Massel Smith

CHAPTER 38
A LETTER TO MYSELF

Dear Massell,

The years go by fast, only yesterday I was twenty.

Today I am seventy-three. Where have those years gone? I see them as a big race. If I knew what I know now, would that have made a difference; I will never know.

Experience comes from learning and time waits for no one. To make dreams come true you have to live your dreams put yourself in those dreams. Take the bull by the horn. Sometimes a little selfishness does no harm. Think of yourself first. Time passes and will never come back.

As I sit here in the twilight hour the gentle breeze brushes my cheeks. Would it have made a difference I will never know? If I had taken what was mine. Time teaches wisdom and understanding. Today I am glad. I let time ran its race.

My regrets are small my joys have out-number them. When I look back on my days living with Aunty Kathleen, I remember the day she told me I was a nobody and I would not amount to anyone. Today no tears come to my eyes. That chapter is long-time closed, and I can lift my head high and I know that no one can ever make me feel that small ever again.

Those words that were uttered to me in anger have been my strength and courage to achieve my dreams and to move forwards. I realize when something is said in anger use it in a way that makes the good in you shine throughout your life.

I know this for sure: If Aunty Kathleen was alive, she would be proud of me.

CHAPTER 39
THE JOURNEY TO SURGERY

When it was time for me to go operating room, a very tall and huge orderly came to escort me. As I walked with him, he adjusted his steps, so that I could keep up with him.

As I walked down in this endless corridor, I could hear a bird chirping. The early morning sun shone on the well-groomed green lawn. My heart refused to acknowledge it. The tears in my eyes, I was fighting to keep them there. As I walked beside this orderly, I appeared composed, but in truth, I was scared, frightened and alone. I thought this must be how one feels when one makes his or her last walk before life is snapped away.

Life changes for everyone. Our past molds the future and the present shapes it. I say this with sincerity. As I look back on my life. I ask myself how did I get to where I am today? I draw strength from my yesterdays. My tomorrows are not promised to me. So, I lived in the now. Each now will be my today's past and each past are yesterday's future. My sisters were not allowed to take that walk with me.

In the pre-operating room, I was as cold as ice. I could feel my bones trembling. Two toasty warm blankets were put over me. As I lay there my mind took me back to the day in the chief an anesthetist's office. He was telling me the different kind of anesthesia. I turned to him and said. "Are you going to put me to sleep?" He paused for jus a moment. The expression on his face was priceless, and then said "Lady! It is not a wart we are removing from your finger!" As I lay there, I thought "What a silly question"

As they wheeled me into the operating room, I could see my sisters looking at me. They were very worried. And they were trying so hard for me not to see. The last thing I remember was the anesthetist saying, "Think happy thoughts." And then I was out.

Massel Smith

Everything was in a haze. I could hear someone calling me. "Massell! Wake up, it is time to wake up." Then I will drift off once more.

My Mother Sleeps

CHAPTER 40
THE APHASIA INSTITUTE AND PAT ARATO CENTRE

What it has done for me.
I know a place which is the Aphasia Institute and Pat Arato Center.
A brain tumor as its way to make one feel helpless and lost.
After surgery to remove the tumor, my life took on a new phase.
I had never heard of the word Aphasia before, but I would soon find out
I was lost within myself.

But I would soon find a place that would let me see my glass half full.
This place the Aphasia Institute was recommended to me by my speech
Language Pathologist, "The Aphasia Institute and the Pat Arato Centre".
Oh what a place; it took me from darkness and into the light.
What a blessing I came the Centre with broken wings and it as showed me that I can still fly.

Massel Smith

CHAPTER 41
MY APHASIA AND ME

From the glory of the sunset, to the fresh morning dew.
The unique of experience being alive.
Aphasia! What crowded mind, unscrambled thoughts the future looks grim, uncertainty sets in, but the intelligent mind refuses to cave in.
So, the struggles go on day after day.
As courage endure and inner strengths shines through.

Aphasia! Never stop learning as babies do.
Laughter fills the room as funny gestures and sounds act out words in my head Elated, I stand!
Joyful sounds and cheers can be heard all around, as successfully my challenges are met
Aphasia! One message clear.
Experiences in giving is pure and a delightful joy.
Receiving is equal and a bless from above so thanks,

Is forever spoken by these lips.
It's the love and caring.
Sent from the heart
And smiles that shine through
The receiving heart
Aphasia! Humiliation you bring
My eyes are red, my cheeks are wet
Angry words burst forth as tears flow
Why should I be ashamed?
Yet you are here to stay
But my stubborn will, restored self-confidence invisible though you are
Our lives are entwine as long as I live
Me and my Aphasia.

My Mother Sleeps

CHAPTER 42
A JOURNEY THROUGH THE FOREST

It was early evening there was a nice cool breeze that put me in the mood of relaxation. I was completely relaxed. I must have fallen asleep, for I was in this forest, the sun was shining through the trees as they dance to the music of the breeze. The ground was damp, but fresh. I could hear the singing of the birds and my heart was filled with joy.

As I walked among the trees, I could see a rabbit ahead of me hopping ahead of me on path made by the many visitors. The rabbit was gray and white, very chubby. This made me think of Easter. As I continued my walk, I could hear some movement among the trees. I looked up and there was a monkey swinging from branch to branch. Entertaining me with his acrobatics, I could not help but smile. As he did his tricks, he would make funny sounds. I stopped to take a good look and to listen to his chatter. He was light brown, on his feet was a ribbon of white, it looked as if someone had painted that ribbon of white. As I stood there watching it came to my mind how could one think that human came from monkeys. Yes, they do things that human do, but surely, we are not from monkeys. I took a deep breath and move on.

The sun was getting warmer as afternoon turned into evening. I was feeling a bit tired. I need to fine a place to rest my tired feet. I needed a drink of cool water, but I did not take water I forgot. Ahead I could see a huge pine tree, I will just sit there for a while it looks welcoming. As I got closer to the tree, I notice a fox sleeping. Was he really sleeping or was he looking for a meal? I was not going to wait to find out. This big brown and gray fox were not going to have launch at my expense.

My rest was over, time has come I should move on. As I walked further in the forest I could here the sound of my steps on the dry leaves, the soft music of the wind and the sweet chirping of the birds. Then, as to rob me of this special time I heard a haunting call of the owl. I looked up at the tree to see the owl.

There was a flash of light that looked like crystal in the sun light. This took my breath away then as the branch swayed in the gently breeze and the sun came peeping through once more. The crystal rose to the occasion. There was something about this glow. It was as if it was calling me. My eyes follow this glow to the base of the tree, which was shining bright and polling me to it. I saw a key at first, I thought someone had dropped their golden key. I stopped to pick it up; with my fingers curled around it I thought this is a special key. It was no ordinary key, it did not just fall, it was placed there. For me to find. I have seen the like of such a key before. It was beautiful extremely beautiful. There were engravings like stars. As I held it the sun worked its magic. I felt this key had a message or massages for me, I must receive it. Knock and it shall open unto you. Seek and he shall find. Be still my soul and know you are not alone. There is a light above you that will light your way.

I was on top of the world, with the key in my hand, my fingers encircled it. I felt warm with excitement as I continued my walk. There was a big tree ahead its branches hung like tear drops. There is something about the Weeping Willow that make you shed a few tears at times.

At first, I did not see the vase that was place under the Weeping Willow. It was white bone china trimmed with gold. On the sides were angles, their hands were clasped as if they were praying. It was adorned with delicate pink lilies and white daises. The feeling of peace came over me. I lift my head to the heaven and gave thanks to the One that created me.

My walk took me farther in the forest. As I walked, I was looking around to see if animals were lurking in the grass or behind the trees. As the tallgrass swayed in the breeze, I caught sight of a black patch among the tall grass. Getting closer I could see it was a bear. My heart stared beating faster and faster, I wanted to scream. But I had to control myself. Should I run, or act as if I did not see him and hope he did not see me. Finally, I was out of his sight and I felt safe once more.

My Mother Sleeps

I was coming to the end of the forest, there were tall grass almost as tall as me they were different shades of green, creating a tapestry woven by mother nature. There were no dark clouds in the sky. Each blade of grass dance to the gentle music of the wind. Then as they sway this way and that, I caught sight of a sheet of sparkling diamonds on a sheet of blue satin. What a picture, no human hands could create. Mother nature was in her glory. I reach out and gave God the praise. I kept walking I was coming to the end of the forest. Before me was the bed the sparking bed of diamonds. There were no movements on the lake, just the elusion of a bed sparking diamond. The beautiful blue sky creates elusion of the diamonds. I took a deep breath; I could stay here forever. This beauty will never leave me. It will stay until I am dead. (This world is not my home I am only passing through.)

As I walked along the shore of the lake, I thought I must get to the other side. But how, I do not swim. "How does one get over there, there must be a way?" I kept hoping I would find a way. Then I asked myself this question, "Am I ready to cross over?" I was not ready; for once, I am over to the other side I cannot come back.

In life there are so much to learn. In my journey through the forest, my mind was open to learn from nature. There are so much to learn from little things like the rabbit. I see myself as being shy. Very careful. Monkey loves to talk; some people may see me wanting to know everything and going the extra mile.

Like in the case of the fox. I can say I worked very hard. I don't let things keep me down. The key needed to tell me I can-not give up.
In the case of the Vase or the Vessel, my faith is strong, and without that faith, that faith I would not be here today.
The bear is very determined I am just like that bear. I will fight for what I stand for.

The barrier is talking about death that is something one cannot rush. In this journey in the forest brings together Human, Animals and Mother Nature. The living and the death the complete circle.

Massel Smith

CHAPTER 43
A ROSE GARDEN

What a beautiful thought, not just a thought but a beauty to behold.
A rose garden cannot shine without care, dedication and the right nourishment.
Plant me a rose and then turn your back.
Will that rose grow?
Will it shine and fill the space around it with pleasant exotic aroma.
What we are doing here today and for the past year Is supplying some nourishment.
That the air will be filled with pleasant aroma.
Each rose will make its own mark.
What you are willing to do is a blessing to you, the giver and to the receiver.
We are saying to the receiver we care.
Let me help you water that garden.
The rose garden will not grow without water.
So let me lend a hand to give each
Plant a chance to grow not just today, but for the future.
Filling the garden with bright beautiful roses of all different colours and exotic perfume.
This act of love and caring is a blessing to all.
THE ROSE GARDEN.

CHAPTER 44
THIS IS THE TIME SPRING

This the time to awake from slumber and spread joy to all.
This is a time when life is moving around us
A time when rivers, brooks, springs and lakes are alive once more.
The trees that had shed their leaves are now alive and in full bloom.
What joy is given to us human, joy unspeakable to see this miracle of life around us
To hear the birds singing in the trees as they perched on their naked branches.

Squirrels are out of there hiding place and enjoying the beauty of spring.
Look around and see the trees in many shades of green to see the beauty of spring.
Is to see the cherry blossoms in full blooms there are no words to exclaim their beauty.
The peaches, apples, plums, pears and many other trees.
The different color of magnolia- - so vibrant and yet so delicate.
The tulips forget- me- not's, asters and many other flowering trees..

The Forsythia are showing off its magnificent spender of bright yellow.
The weeping willow is getting ready to shelter us from the blazing sun this is what spring is made of.

Massel Smith

TO THE VOLUNTEERS

Volunteers! Oh, Volunteers! what a wonderful sound
It's like music to our ears
How can you hear those sounds?
It's in the smiles on our faces.
Its in the brightness of our eyes.
It's in the words we struggle with.
You have given your time voluntarily,
Asking nothing in return.
Your patience is beyond words.
You have made us the members, see that
Life is bigger than Aphasia.
You have exemplified the true meaning
Of Volunteer.
I will always thank you throughout my
Life journey.

TO MY READERS

One of my dreams is to see the world all of it. I have seen a great deal but not all of it. Give me the strength and the courage to look ahead and move on. I believe when one door closes another will open. I see my glass as half full never half empty. The past has given me the will to move on. Each day is a new one. Yesterday is gone never to return. My life is a tapestry woven by the Master's hands I see the light never the dark. I gravitate to the light never the dark.

I love to read, another one of my dreams is to write for children. One day I will see all of these come through. I never see my glass as half empty; I see it as half full.

Massel Smith

Valerie, my dear sister Valerie. Far too soon you became a Mother.
Those were the days you should have been playing with your
dolls or doing the things a ten-year old do., in
a mother for your brothers and sisters.

You did this with a smile . you never put yourself first.
How can I say thanks? There are no word or words enough to say thanks.

Your youth was taken from you. Yet you never showed any signs of strain.
To care for us was all you knew. If Mama could see you, she would be so proud of you.

Dear sister of mine I love you so much .
You were always there .. We could talk with you and you would listen. You always have an answer. You never asked for much.

May your life be full of happiness.
Take care precious one.
I love you.

ACKNOWLEDGEMENT

Thanks to You All. You have encouraged me all the way Michael Wiley, Joshuas Ekeanyanwu and my dear friend Mary. Thanks, and more thanks to each one.

To the WorkBook Press:
Mr. Paul Stewart and His Team for a job Well done. I thank you all very much, Keep up the good work.

www.ingramcontent.com/pod-product-compliance
Lightning Source LLC
Chambersburg PA
CBHW052120110526
44592CB00013B/1686